Let's face it, we've all failed. Maybe not on a grand scale, but in some way, shape or form, we've screwed up.

And unless you're hopelessly narcissistic, you've probably referred to yourself as a failure at one time or another.

So what do we all mean when we say something or someone is a *failure*?

The dictionary definition is *lack of success*. In other words, everything from *flop* to *disaster* and all points in between.

But what happens if we take this short-sighted view of failure and flip it on its head? What if we re-imagine failure as one of the surest routes to creative success, instead of the road to perdition? Perhaps the mistakes and circumstances that join forces to create failure are not your mortal enemy but are, in fact, the key elements in producing something new and exciting.

If there's one thing a thirty-year career in the creative industry has taught me, it's that no one is immune to failure. You might be brilliant and successful, beautiful and talented, but no one can placate the gods of success for ever.

Pretty much everyone who has ever tried anything has cupboards full of botched attempts, rejection letters and memories of being passed over and ignored.

Me, personally? I've screwed up as an artist and designer. I've screwed up as an art director. I've screwed up as a photographer, editor and curator. If I've tried it, I've screwed it up.

I've spent decades watching – and helping – big advertising agencies peddle their diluted versions of perfection. I'm intimately familiar with conventional wisdom's path to stultifying boredom: boring buildings, boring billboards, boring design, boring people.

Avoiding mistakes by not taking risks might not draw the wrath of your boss or client, but it also doesn't draw excess praise. Far too often, playing it safe results in shiny, swirling, bland masses of 'meh'.

These major and minor catastrophes I'm referring to aren't mere learning experiences – after which wrongs are righted, instruments are recalibrated, courses are reset – but are themselves early brushes with success.

And I'm not alone in abandoning the pointless quest for perfection. In the following pages, I've gathered together some of my favourite work by artists and photographers, amateurs and autodidacts, who bask in the glory of imperfection, rule breaking, and show us that right can be

wrong, bad can be good and, when everything tells you to turn right, you might be better served by turning left.

This is a book about having the courage to fail spectacularly when the alternative is boring conformity and dull ideas. It's about rejecting the safe and expected in favour of the exciting and unknown.

This book is dedicated to the art of making mistakes.

The Epic
Fail.

The Happy
Failure.

Fail to Follow the Rules.

Fail to Find Inspiration.

All Hail the Fail.

Complete and total
failure when success
was easily attainable.

The Epic

Fail.

Your mistakes

could change the world.

Small mistakes are part of everyday life. We dial the wrong number. We forget to pay a bill. We call a colleague by the wrong name. These are inconsequential, unavoidable and instantly forgettable errors.

Forget those for a moment and let's imagine the colossal, catastrophic failure. The kind of mistake that can be seen from space. The kind of failure so horrifying that it's preceded by an ominous adverb.

The *epic* fail.

The epic fail is a blunder that makes jaws drop, stomachs churn and empires fall. These are the blunders that break careers and spirits. If caught on video, this fail will spread like a bush fire across social media, landing a coveted spot on epicfail.com.

But the epic fail isn't always an unmitigated disaster, nor is it the exclusive domain of the loser. As I said at the start, even the most successful aren't immune.

Take Apple, the very avatar of a successful company. When Apple rolls out a product that flops – epically or otherwise – it's an event so anomalous that the Earth freezes on its axis, nerd support groups spontaneously form, investors look

on in slack-jawed wonderment. It happened in 2012, when Apple CEO Tim Cook evicted Google Maps from all Apple devices and tasked his team with re-mapping the world.

Then the first reviews came in.

Apple's attempt at cartography resulted in roads shooting up the sides of buildings, tower blocks melting into the pavement and highways folded like origami.

It was an epic failure.

But this fiasco may yet lead to some future success. It seems unlikely, but the future is uncertain, such things are unpredictable and it has happened before.

In 1993 Apple released the Newton to much fanfare, an expensive and clunky handheld computer called a 'personal digital assistant'. The first PDA. It was immediately ridiculed by critics and consumers as extravagant, expensive and unnecessary – an *epic failure* before *epic failures* were even a thing.

But few of those mocking Apple's misfire realized that the device would presage the smartphone and tablet revolution, leading *Wired* magazine

to posthumously praise the Newton PDA as a 'prophetic failure'.

As the writer William Gass observed, 'sometimes accidents happen and beauty is born'. Beauty was indeed born with the ugly Newton.

A certain kind of gastronomic beauty was also born when a morphine-addicted pharmacist went in search of an elixir to rid him of a crippling drug problem. Instead, he became the lucky pharmacist who created Coca-Cola.

The medical world changed for ever when Professor Wilson Greatbatch was building a device to record heart rhythms. He inserted the wrong electrical resistor and watched as the device pulsed, stopped and pulsed again – like a heart. The pacemaker was a screw up that would ultimately save millions of lives.

These aren't uncommon stories. And they illustrate an important lesson: don't coddle your ideas hoping to avoid an epic fail, because the annals of invention are filled with beautiful mistakes.

FAIL FASTER

Just because something doesn't fulfil its original purpose, just because your initial calculations were off by a few degrees, doesn't mean the unexpected result won't lead to something resembling genius.

Celebrate

the illogical.

Today's urban landscapes are studies in uniformity and repetition. The same stores. The same signs. Identical high streets, cafés and shopping malls. Interchangeable parks.

But look closer, look in that sliver of space between H&M and McDonald's and you'll see breaks in the repetition, little colonies of the irrational disrupting the sameness. The balcony with no door. The backwards bench. Bizarre bathrooms.

These are the lapses that make the mundane fascinating, flights of illogic that produce a peculiar, imperfect beauty. And over time, the conspicuous fuck up becomes part of the landscape, an embarrassing mistake that seems just right in its place.

Daniel Eatock, Vandalized Trees Reoriented, 2008

Screw up.

Stand out.

How many times have you heard the mindless call that to achieve greatness you must be willing to 'give 110 per cent'. Everyone's favourite mathematical impossibility suggests that if we throw every ounce of our energy into a project, perfection will follow.

Nonsense. If you want to get noticed, do yourself a favour and *stop* pursuing perfection, because that's exactly what everyone else is doing.

Pursue the imperfect instead.

Something unexpected or surprising is far more memorable than perfection. Look at the billboard on the next page.

Would you really register yet another bland billboard? Well, you might not if it hadn't been jumbled by inattentive workers.

Wage war on your instincts and indulge in the potential beauty of the unforced error. Try creating something virtually perfect. The most beautiful picture you've ever painted. A stunning flower arrangement. The perfect soufflé.

Just when you think you're finished, let it go. Drop the soufflé. Let the neighbour's kid put the final touches on the flower arrangement. Finish the canvas blindfolded.

You might end up with something useless. But you might instead find order in the disorder. A striking abstraction. An unknown sensory experience.

In fact, you just might discover the imperfect perfection of the planned unplanned and the expected unexpected.

There was never a plan. There was just a series of mistakes.

Robert Caro, journalist

Even robots

make
mistakes.

Whether planned or unplanned, mistakes force us to take a closer look – they catch our attention in a sea of bland excellence.

Take the manufacturer's production line, for example, designed to eliminate errors and make imperfections obsolete.

In the past when products were handmade, they often included small variations in quality or minor differences in construction. And then the robots took over, making everything, well, a bit more perfect.

But even robots revolt occasionally.

Artist Heike Bollig has collected a series of familiar objects that have been deformed by their machine creators. The pretzel that refuses to knot. The labels bunched around a jar's middle like a tutu. The unscrewable screw. The unrollable marble. The teabag you can steep from six blocks away.

The fact that they're manufacturing errors only makes these failures more poignant.

They ask us to grapple with complex questions such as: 'If a pretzel doesn't knot, is it still a pretzel? Or is it just a Twiglet?'

It's occasionally worth switching off our own quality control to let some oddballs through.

Heike Bollig, Jar. Found in Stockholm, 2008

nationen dieser acht Symbole bilden das
er 64 Kapitel des *Buchs der Wandlungen*.
ng beruht denn auch auf der Nebeneinan-
hrer symbolischen Werte:
ymbolisiert *Stärke* oder *Kreativität*.
olisiert *Freude* oder *Anziehung*.
ymbolisiert *Initiative* oder *Handeln*.
nbolisiert *Aufmerksamkeit* oder
sein.
bolisiert *Empfänglichkeit* oder
heit.
bolisiert *Innehalten* oder *Ruhe*.
mbolisiert *Leidenschaft* oder *Gefahr*.
mbolisiert *Eindringen* oder *Nachfolgen*.
ragung wird ein Symbolpaar ausgewählt,
aften repräsentiert, die die betreffende Si-
akterisieren. Diese Eigenschaften können
der Persönlichkeit und des Charakters ein-
chen oder Gruppen stehen, genauso aber
dominanten Kräfte, die ein Ereignis, eine
er ein Unterfangen charakterisieren.
bolpaar ergibt zwei Hexagramme (oder ein
, bei dem dasselbe Symbol zweimal ge-
d). Diese bilden den Text für die Befragung
in der weiter unten beschriebenen Art und
n. Benützen Sie bitte die Tabelle hinten auf
as die Kombinationen der Trigramme und
mme, die sie bilden, betrifft. Die ange-
piele am Ende der Einführung zeigen typi-

11

Heike Bollig, Book. Found at University Bookshop Munich, 2004.

ches Symbol nicht für das männliche Ge...
steht nicht für die Frau und Yang nicht für...
Yin und Yang sind universelle Komplemen...
len Menschen und allen Ereignissen vorhan...

Es ist außerdem wichtig zu verstehen, ...
Yang nicht gut beziehungsweise schlecht re...
Yin und Yang können sowohl gut als auch s...
je nachdem, welche Funktion die jeweilige...
in einer bestimmten Situation hat.

3. Die »vier Bilder« heißen altes (reifes, ...
junges (kleines) Yin und Yang. Der Yin-M...
terteilt in altes Yin und junges Yang, auch...
punkt zustrebendes Yin oder anfänglich...
nannt. Der Yang-Modus ist unterteilt in al...
junges Yin, auch dem Höhepunkt zustre...
und anfängliches Yin genannt.

Diese Unterteilungen verdeutlichen das ...
die Yin- und Yang-Erscheinungsformen d...
sches sind, sondern sich immer in einem Pro...
nehmens oder Abnehmens befinden.

4. Die »acht Trigramme«, die aus den viere...
Yin und Yang entstehen, vervollständigen r...
gende Struktur des *Buchs der Wandlungen* ...
jene Symbole, die zur schnellen Befragung...
verwendet werden:

Alte Yang-Trigramme: HIMMEL und SEE...
Junge Yin-Trigramme: DONNER und FEU...
Alte Yin-Trigramme: ERDE und BERG...
Junge Yang-Trigramme: WASSER und WI...

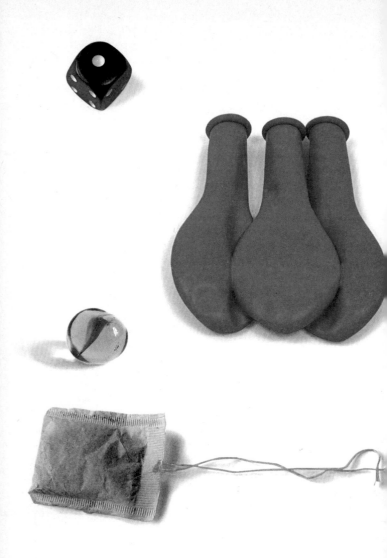

Heike Bollig, Dice. Found in a board game box, 2006
3 pink balloons. Received from Yuka Oyama, 2005
Marble. Manufacturer unknown, 2009

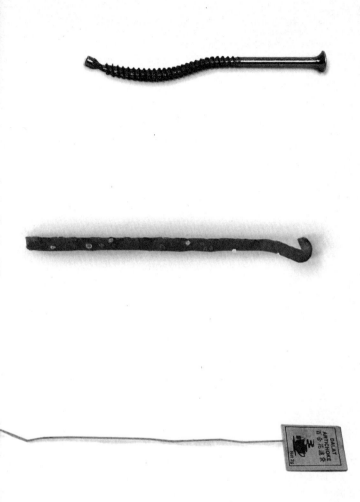

Screw. Found at Obi, Munich, 2004
Pretzel stick. Received from Jürgen Drescher, 2006
Teabag. Found at a Vietnamese grocer's shop, Berlin, 2005

Triumph

of the amateur.

You may, or may not, remember the days when the work of amateur photographers remained at home, pasted in photo albums and stored in cardboard boxes, each a gallery of bland and often accidentally experimental photography.

Apart from those gruelling slide shows of your neighbour's trip to Albania, personal photographs tended to be intimate and private.

But the ubiquity of smartphones and digital cameras has brought the amateur photograph online and into the mainstream, providing lessons for professionals in the process.

An amateur's gift is naivety.

If you don't know the rules, you don't know not to break them. The amateur doesn't fear failure.

They have no preconceptions, no clients and no deadlines. They don't necessarily follow trends and can afford to root around in the deeply unusual for brilliance, even if they don't always recognize when they've found it.

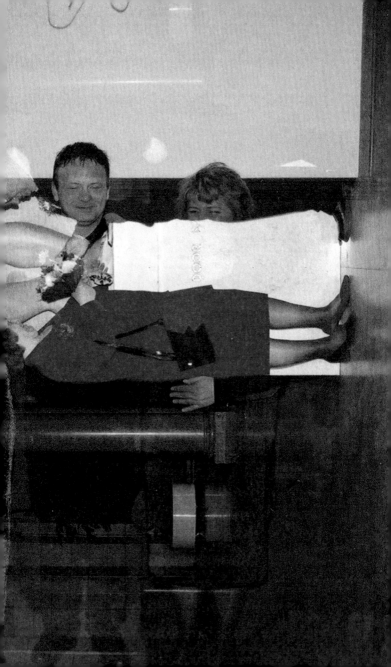

Sure, there are more bad pictures than good, but what many professionals might see as photographic defeat — blurred focus, subjects cut off at the ankles and squinting into the sunlight, lamp posts growing out of heads — can in fact be a potent source of inspiration. These are the kind of things professionals toss in the trash and families send out as holiday cards.

Most creative professionals look to fellow professionals for inspiration. But when ideas are borrowed, modified and cannibalized from within, they are rarely innovative or original.

Amateurs tend not to be slavish about getting the picture 'right', they just want to get the picture. They are not saddled with ideas of 'artistic precedent' or 'creative vision'.

They never know what they might end up with, and they don't particularly care.

Nor should you.

Ever tried.
Ever failed.
No matter.
Try again.
Fail again.
Fail better.

Samuel Beckett, playwright

Attack of

the giant
finger.

Admit it. Everyone does it. If anything, as cameras get smaller, the risk gets bigger.

It is the single most common fuck up in photography: the wayward photographer's finger that, like a surprise eclipse, partially obscures the subject. If the finger is a photographer's most essential tool, the finger-over-the-lens shot transforms a ruined picture into a self-portrait.

Before digital cameras made costly film processing irrelevant, when we paid for each finger-on-the-lens failure, we lived amongst these images. All of us amateurs of a certain vintage have a photo lurking in the back of a drawer of a friend or loved one standing on the Place de la Concorde, beheaded by a fat index finger.

The results range from the charmingly awful to the disconcertingly creepy. A pinkish corona in the sky. The erasure of a single face in a group photo, like a purged comrade in a Soviet newspaper. A tantalizing glimpse of a location. A beautiful, Rothko-like abstraction created by blocks of blurred pinks.

Today these images are more likely to be deleted than saved, and if you ask me, that's a shame.

This is not to say that you should *deliberately* obscure the camera's lens. It's impossible to intentionally reproduce an accidental effect.

But a photograph with an imperfection you only notice later isn't necessarily ruined.

It isn't necessarily a failure. It's just the starting point for something else.

Confidence is

overrated.

We all like to project confidence. We think we *must* project confidence. We assume it's a prerequisite of success.

But when it comes to creativity, it's actually insecurity that's essential.

Don't believe me?

What trait do you most associate with history's celebrated artists? Happiness, confidence and self-satisfaction? Or depression, self-hatred and misery? Would *The New York Times* have recently wondered if 'self-loathing is a requirement for writers' if success demanded confidence?

No, because they understand that great ideas are often germinated by crippling insecurity. Great ideas come from doubting them, interrogating them and allowing other possibilities to take root.

It can be a risky business, all this thinking, but take the risk. The creative process is like panning for gold: there might be a nugget in there somewhere and it's your job to get on your hands and knees and sift through the dirt and grime to find it. And the moment you're absolutely 110 per cent sure you've hit gold is probably the moment to think about panning somewhere else.

I'm not talking about hurling babies out with old bathwater. It could be as simple as a change of lighting. A new viewpoint. Adjusting a concept or altering an angle. It's admitting that there's probably room for improvement, or even that you might just be entirely wrong.

Don't let your insecurities overwhelm you. And most importantly, don't panic.

Insecurity is one of your most valuable assets.

Thinking is hard. Not thinking is harder.

Hans Aarsman, photographer

**Opportunity wears
many disguises.
Be on the lookout.**

The Happy
Failure.

Sharpen

your gaze.

Serendipity. It sounds wonderful.

And there's something so romantic in the idea of coincidence, happenstance, luck.

You might even take comfort in believing that you have no control over moments of inspiration. That it happens irrespective of your actions and it's out of your hands.

What Matt Stuart's and André Thijssen's photography reminds us about serendipity is that you can — and in fact need to — work at it. Most of those moments we call serendipitous are in fact just about keeping your eyes open.

Stuart might seem to have a knack for being in the right place at the right time. But in reality, he's constantly on the hunt for those juxtapositions, oddities and disconnections that thousands of people pass by without noticing.

An elegant peacock is turned into a rubber duck. A New York cop becomes a member of the Village People. A pigeon joins the morning commute.

Matt Stuart, Moorgate Tube, 2005

Trafalgar Square, 2004

New Bond Street, 2006

Hyde Park, 2006

Matt Stuart, Fifth Avenue, 2010

Thijssen scours the periphery of daily life to find beauty, and often humour, in hidden or overlooked corners and mundane locations. He seeks out visual moments that transform the ordinary into the memorable.

Learn to recognize these transformative moments. Don't dismiss the imperfect, the unphotogenic, the 'ugly'. Because inspiration is just as likely to be found there.

Remember all the beautiful movements initially dismissed as alien and ugly: Abstraction, Dadaism, Punk, Grunge, the razor-blade gargling perfection of Tom Waits's voice.

Scrutinizing your surroundings might not be an instinct, but it can become a skill. Switch off your automatic pilot. Head up from your mobile phone. Slow down a little and sharpen your gaze. Even if you are searching for the unexpected, it will always surprise you.

You can't predict the unexpected, but you can learn to recognize it.

André Thijssen, Tree and building, Malaga, Spain, 2013

André Thijssen, Mirror, Rosh Pina, Namibia, 2000

André Thijssen, Car with Balls, USA, 2002

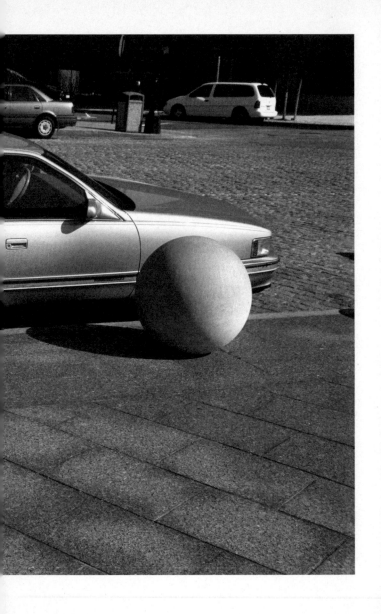

Make mistakes.

Every day.

Making a mistake is normal. Making the same mistake twice is careless. Making it three times borders on the inexcusable.

But making the same mistake over and over and over again can approach genius.

If we learn from our mistakes, it follows that we learn most when our mistakes become our obsessions, when we're so determined to overcome them that we repeat, repeat and repeat. It's an instinct often avoided by professionals, with their emphasis on competence and perfectionism, and their focus on deadlines and demanding clients.

Let's again snatch an example from the hands of the professional and put it into the bumbling hands of the amateur.

A common challenge that has long plagued amateur photographers – those unfamiliar with the f-stop, baffled by ISO settings, mystified by the light meter – is shooting something jet black. Now, imagine that this object is an undifferentiated puff of blackness, with no contours and no shades, and one that refuses to keep still.

One intrepid amateur photographer tried year after year to take a picture of his beloved pet.

And year after year he failed.

The photos were punctuated by a mysterious black circle. Sometimes a blurry black triangle. Occasionally a black hole. But the photographer's persistence is a moving testament to the relationship between a pet and his owners.

It's an epic story of love, obsession, perseverance and bad lighting.

One error, repeated ad infinitum, made the dog invisible. And then, quite unexpectedly and by means of another error, we see at last what all the fuss was about.

In one last attempt, likely born out of pure frustration, the loving owners over-exposed an image of their dog.

Finally they captured the pet's features in detail, revealing a slightly bored creature that looks pretty much like every other black dog.

Clarity turned out to be quotidian. It's the mistake, that flash of blackness, the dog we can't see that sparks the imagination.

The tyranny

of perfection.

Do this. Don't do that. Concentrate on this. Ignore that. Work longer. Work harder.

We've all been overwhelmed by well-intentioned advice that borders on the belligerent, meant to aim us towards the perfect.

But let's consider that actually the opposite might be more helpful. This quote, attributed to (but probably never said by) Salvador Dalí: 'Have no fear of perfection. You'll never reach it.'

Or this one from plain-speaking American football coach Vince Lombardi: 'We are going to relentlessly chase perfection, knowing full well we will not catch it ... In the process we will catch excellence.'

Since we're wading through the swamp of inspirational platitudes, remember that these are just elegant examples of famous people re-stating another useful cliché: don't make the perfect the enemy of the good.

Striving for perfection will make you uncomfortable. It will make you feel like shit about your own fuck ups. And who are we kidding? Imperfection is always closer to reality.

If you're paying attention, and not moaning about all of life's cruelties and petty injustices, there's *always* something you can learn from it.

Perfect *is* the enemy of the good. Free yourself from the tyranny of perfection! Never surrender!

We are all failures – at least the best of us are.

J. M. Barrie, author

When a view is flawless,

interrupt it.

Unless you're reading this at home, you're probably on camera. Webcams are everywhere. They're all-seeing. In the park. At the bar. In the library stacks. They line city streets and hover in the skies.

Webcams have transformed the world into something that Winston Smith could never have imagined. In some ways, today's Big Brother is more benign, but everywhere you go, the electronic Stasi is watching you.

Even if no one is actually watching.

Like production-line robots, webcams might not appear to offer much in the way of creative inspiration. They dispassionately monitor nearly everything and almost nothing: traffic flows, tourist

locations, beautiful landscapes and street corners. And yet all of nature's unguarded moments and chance wonders are collected, recorded and saved.

Kurt Caviezel has spent fifteen years monitoring 15,000 webcams from all over the world. But he wasn't interested in the endless, tedious hours of the picturesque and perfect. Instead he was looking for the interrupted view, the moments when something unexpected happens.

In Caviezel's world, the agents of disruption are giant insects, hovering above the pyramids of Giza like a B-movie nightmare. The heavens darken when a bird's tail blots out the sky. The fragile world appears constantly under threat. Cameras installed as a means of observation and security against menace become a vehicle for creativity and menace.

Caviezel has the webcam beat covered, but his lesson is a valuable one: be on the lookout for intrusions and visual anomalies, even when you least expect them.

The blot on the landscape might just change the way you see the world.

Kurt Caviezel, Insects

Kurt Caviezel, Insects

Kurt Caviezel, Birds

Rules are made to be broken. Don't just bend them. Smash them. Blow them up. Destroy them.

Fail to Follow the Rules.

Redesign your

imagination.

These days it seems that everything, everywhere is the same.

There's a Starbucks on every corner in Manhattan and London. There's one at the Louvre in Paris, at the Guantanamo Bay prison camp and inside a South Carolina funeral home.

And it's not just coffee shops and chain stores. It's everything. The same doormats, shoes, plugs, condiments, coffee makers are everywhere.

The scenery of life appears as one continuous backdrop, no matter where you are.

Italian designer Daniele Pario Perra challenges this notion by deliberately using things in the 'wrong' way. He approaches common products with an open, if slightly demented, mind and finds new uses for them: an electrical socket becomes a candle holder, film canisters are remodelled as salt and pepper shakers, and a plastic chair becomes a makeshift bicycle seat.

Daniele Pario Perra, Low Cost Design, 2010–11

Artist Helmut Smits is in the business of creating unholy alliances.

His Chairlight shows that sometimes the results can be playful, charming *and* actually useful.

The artist collective PUTPUT also rewrites the rules by marrying ideas, areas and objects that are at odds with each other. Common household objects are forced to procreate, forming a beautifully impractical new object.

Forget what you know about objects.

Look at them afresh and discover new potential, because nothing will limit your creativity more than sticking to what is appropriate or usual.

Helmut Smits, Chairlight, 2006

PUTPUT, Fitting 01

Fitting 03

Put the puzzle back

the
wrong way.

You'd be forgiven for thinking there's not much one can learn from piecing together a massive jigsaw puzzle that, when completed, reveals a cheerful unicorn in repose.

Perhaps they're challenging for children, but for almost everyone else they're merely a perfect image disassembled, only to be reassembled into its perfect state. And there isn't much mystery involved, either: the target image of the completed puzzle is always printed on the lid of the box.

Perfection, fragmentation, perfection. It's a satisfying sequence.

But not for American artist Kent Rogowski.

He realized that some puzzle companies use the same die-cut patterns to create all of their puzzles – making the pieces interchangeable between puzzles, whatever the picture. Rogowski used this exact correspondence to blend different puzzles, combining disparate images.

The results are startlingly beautiful: bucolic wonderlands where flowers burst in colourful blooms from landscapes, out of buildings and from the sides of animals.

Perfection, fragmentation, stunning *imperfection*. Now that's the more satisfying sequence.

Carve things up. Break things down. Scatter the pieces. Throw away the instructions and put the pieces back together in whatever way you damn well please, all the while remembering that things that aren't meant to go together can still work together.

And like Rogowski, you might end up with a creation that is *technically* wrong, but aesthetically just right.

Kent Rogowski, Love = love 9, 2006–08

Love = love 3, 2006–08

Kent Rogowski, Love = love 10, 2006–08

Dare to be

disliked.

In this era of Facebook, Twitter and Instagram likes, when the famous and ambitious crave public affirmations from those they barely know, it's important to remember something easily forgotten: a million people can be fantastically wrong.

It's a truism demonstrated every day in bestseller lists, pop-music charts, election results and box-office receipts: there isn't much wisdom in crowds.

But cultural gatekeepers can be astonishingly wrong too.

Think of the countless brilliant ideas first rejected by those trained to spot brilliant ideas. The critics who panned the Impressionists following their first group exhibition. The countless restaurants that

passed on the chance to serve Colonel Sanders's special fried-chicken recipe. The twelve publishers who rejected the first Harry Potter book.

Go against the twin tides of what's popular and the supposed wisdom of trendsetters.

Have the confidence not to care about what other people think.

It's always risky.

We like being in the herd. We like to conform.
We can't help being people pleasers. And original ideas aren't always immediately popular. They'll be questioned, challenged, probed and disassembled.

But if they're good, they'll survive.

Dare to be disliked. You might even like it.

Success is the ability to go from failure to failure without losing your enthusiasm.

Winston Churchill,
former British Prime Minister

Keep it

simple.

Of the many bad traits that plague those of us in the creative world, one of the most damaging is the desire to overcomplicate things.

How many times have you been paralyzed into inaction by minor problems because you demanded an unnecessarily *major* idea to solve it? One of those shit-kicking, jaw-dropping, world-changing *big* ideas?

Stop wasting your time.

You're not going to solve cold fusion every time you slump in front of your computer. Adhere to what engineers call the KISS principle.

Keep It Simple, Stupid.

Ruth van Beek keeps it simple by taking unremarkable photographs and folding them into remarkable surrealistic collages, creating levitating dogs and headless balls of fur.

By manipulating the original images – and without adding any additional elements – she introduces multiple ideas into a single frame.

It's a simple idea with a wonderful result.

Play with something ordinary and make it extraordinary. Don't worry about what you might be destroying; think about what you're creating.

Ruth van Beek, Untitled (The Levitators, 20), 2012–13

Untitled (konijn), 2011

Untitled (grey-black), 2011

Untitled (konijn), 2011

Untitled (dark grey), 2011

Ruth van Beek, Untitled (The Levitators 7), 2012–13

Don't take yourself

too seriously.

The world is full of self-satisfied, self-serious, self-aggrandizers. Despite this surplus of hyper-confident people, you'll often be advised to project more confidence, to display an even more demented sense of determination if you want to vault past your peers.

This is sound advice if you're a politician or a professional wrestler.

For the rest of us, not so much.

A high self-regard and inflated ego can actually limit creativity, as confidence gives way to laziness. You'll roll out the same ideas over and over again, many of them powered by hubris rather than good judgement.

And because even the egotistical don't like an ego-tripping colleague, you'll eventually be brought back to Earth by envious and irritated enemies.

There's no telling *how* the crash will happen, or *when* it will happen, but the self-satisfied and over-confident will always crash. And as you lie twisted and broken in the wreckage, it's here that you'll discover your best ideas.

Because brilliance begins at rock bottom.

**Don't be scared to
sift through your rejects
in search of ideas.**

Fail to Find Inspiration.

Make an

idiot out of yourself.

Making mistakes is part of being human. So why is everyone so resistant to it?

Children learn by trying and failing. Then trying again. And then failing even harder. But children also live in a dream world of play, where mistakes have no consequences, nor are they burdened by the terror of self-consciousness.

So why shouldn't adults do the same? Why shouldn't we learn to play?

If you don't feel like an idiot at least once a day, you need to work less and play more. Dumb errors force us to learn, progress and innovate.

Feel humiliated?

Get used to it.

If you're not making mistakes. If you're not regularly feeling stupid. If you don't believe your ideas are inadequate. If no one is arching an eyebrow while slowly, condescendingly asking why on earth you're doing this. If your ideas aren't routinely mocked when shared with those who follow the rules.

You're probably doing it wrong.

Photoshop doesn't have to mean

perfection.

Gone are the days of processing and slicing film. Anyone can now write, direct and edit a film on their laptop without ever seeing an editing suite. Technology has brought highly specialized skills within everyone's reach.

But access to sophisticated technology doesn't always result in sophisticated thinking.

Technical tricks can enhance good ideas, but more often they just become a way of disguising bad ideas and covering up weaknesses. Projects become driven by execution rather than fully formed concepts.

Tools like Photoshop present yet another danger – nowadays, we can escape all too quickly from our mistakes with just a few keyboard strokes, allowing us to undo a mistake before it even has time to breathe.

Artist Lucas Blalock shows us the opposite: what can happen if you take mistakes as inspiration and allow them to evolve by amplifying something others would strive to hide.

He uses Photoshop to transform technically perfect images into things that are much more interesting, from a mutant cactus to a rocking chair that thinks it's a table.

While commercial photographers use Photoshop to erase and mask imperfection, Blalock introduces imperfection – exposing rather than concealing his interference – to create images that are both striking and unique.

Take time to consider mistakes – both yours and others' – and what you at first see as an error might well be the spark of something else. Something fascinating, strange or original.

Lucas Blalock, Cactus Action, 2014

Lucas Blalock, Tire II, 2011

Rocking Chair, 2012

Keep your audience

audience

on their toes.

There's a predictable uniformity to the family photograph. You know the one. The perfect image of a perfect family – mum, dad, 2.4 kids – in their lovingly furnished home, a carefully crafted scene designed to obscure all of life's imperfections. The grinning boy sits on dad's knee, while his gap-toothed sister presses a chubby little cheek against her mother's smiling face.

That's what the Dutch artist Hans Eijkelboom was looking for when he went into several homes to create his own version of the family portrait.

At first glance the images are exactly what you'd expect – wholesome visions of typical families.

But take a closer look.

Hans Eijkelboom, With My Family, 1973

Hans Eijkelboom, With My Family, 1973

Hans Eijkelboom, With My Family, 1973

That's right, the father in every image is the same man: Hans Eijkelboom.

Photography is not only a form of documentation; it's just as often a tool for manipulation.

Each individual family portrait is entirely believable. Eijkelboom never looks out of place. The persuasiveness of the image allows him to deceive us. And in doing so, he questions our ideas about identity and pokes fun at photographic clichés.

Artist Joan Fontcuberta has worked for years in the borderlands between truth and fiction, science and art, teaching us to question the veracity of what we see while challenging our faith in the idea of 'rules'.

When Fontcuberta announced that he had discovered new constellations overlooked by experts at NASA, critics wondered how the professional astronomers had missed something so important. It was only when viewers saw the final image in the series that Fontcuberta's trickery was revealed. With the right angle, lighting and exposure, he transformed a dirty windscreen into a galaxy far, far away, fooling amateurs and experts alike.

Play with assumptions, make people look and think twice. Truth is there only to be questioned and challenged.

Joan Fontcuberta, MN 3: CANES VENATICI (NGC 5272), AR 16h 42,4 min. / D +28° 23', 1993

Joan Fontcuberta, MN 3: CANES VENATICI (NGC 5272), AR 16h 42,4 min. / D +28º 23', 1993

MN 27: VULPECULA (NGC 6853), AR 19h 56,6 min. / D +22º 43', 1993

Joan Fontcuberta, Car Window, 1993

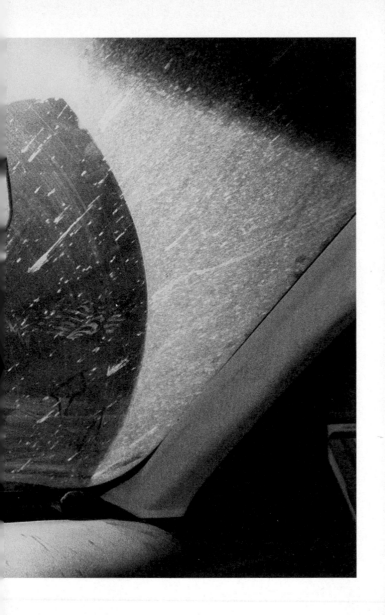

Other people's rejects can

become your masterpiece.

There's a huge amount of waste in the creative process. Rejected ideas. Fruitless brainstorming sessions. Crossed-out pages. For every idea that gets an audition, hundreds are rejected.

But someone else's half-empty trash could become your half-full treasure. Just because something has been rejected by someone doesn't mean it doesn't have potential.

Artist Joachim Schmid revels in found photographs – images that are abandoned, lost or thrown away by their rightful owners.

In his hands, seemingly mundane images, shorn of their contexts and personalities, are transformed into something intriguing.

Here he plays with one of the most predictable of all photographic formats: the studio portrait.

Schmid got hold of a box of rejected negatives, cut in half so they couldn't be used. He noticed that the studio had positioned the lights, camera and subject in exactly the same way for almost every image.

He re-paired the negatives, fitting them together with unfamiliar other halves. The visual fit is almost perfect, the result wonderfully improbable.

Schmid turned a photographer's rejects into his own series of harmonious Franken-portraits.

Just because someone didn't see the potential in their own work doesn't mean you can't. The secret is to approach the creative process with an open mind so that you notice the continuities, correspondences and juxtapositions that others might have missed.

You might just strike the inspirational jackpot.

Joachim Schmid, Photogenetic Drafts #8, 1991

Joachim Schmid, Photogenetic Drafts #15, 1991

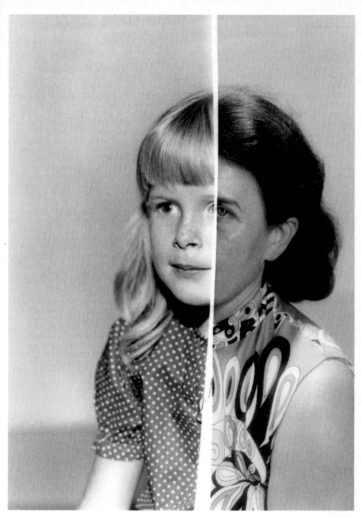

Photogenetic Drafts #24, 1991

Work on your

backyard.

Everyone has a friend with a perfectly manicured front yard – flowers in bright, neat rows, neatly clipped hedges and artfully positioned pots.

But their backyard is the complete opposite: an untidy, neglected mess, with a haphazard jumble of gardening tools, weeds and overgrown plants.

It's a great metaphor for the creative process.

The front yard is the finished work. But it's in the backyard where the real work happens, where you get to wander around in your underwear, muttering to yourself, taking chances, running risks. And without the hard work in the back, the front yard wouldn't even exist.

We all need a place where we can test and develop our ideas before we present them to the world.

It's here you'll begin nurturing the seeds that will one day grow into something ready to put on display for the neighbours.

Failing that, there's always the compost.

Don't

be boring.

Where do you find inspiration? Most of us in the creative world find inspiration in the same places – art galleries, photobooks, movie theatres, websites, magazines, even each other. This tends to lead to uniformity and blandness.

Don't be like everyone else.

That's boring.

Of course, there's plenty to be found in all the usual places, but why limit yourself when the raw material that fuels creativity surrounds you?

German artist Peter Piller finds inspiration in the everyday – and seemingly unpromising – universe of regional newspapers.

It was here that he noticed something curious – hi-vis reflectors sewn into firefighter uniforms.

Peter Piller, Regionale Leuchten, 2005–10

They don't exist as bits of aesthetic flair; they perform a vital safety function in times of emergency. But add a news photographer's flash and they explode: feet in balls of light, glowing breasts, partially alien bodies.

The same mistake is made time and again, transforming serious news images into frames from an old sci-fi movie.

Piller discovers the accidental artistry in images that most would either dismiss as mistakes or, if you're employed by a local newspaper in Germany, not notice at all.

Easily done.

You just have to remember to look.

Failure is the condiment that gives success its flavor.

Truman Capote, author

All Hail
the Fail.

If you're anything like me, you're called an idiot at least once a day.

And that's okay.

Because making mistakes, flirting with disaster and pure, outright failure is how you get better. Without it, you're stuck in a zone of mediocrity and 'meh'. Sure, you probably won't be nervous, self-conscious and potentially mortified, but you won't be admired, either.

You'll be…

Boring.

If you want to be creative, do original work and surprise the hell out of someone every once in a while, you need to get over your fear of looking stupid.

Seek out failure. Train yourself to recognize it all around you. Get to know it and take it away for a romantic weekend.

Failure isn't fatal – quite the contrary.

It's downright fabulous.

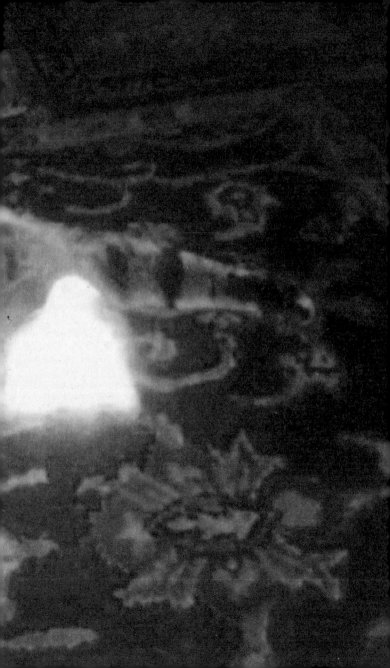

Phaidon Press Limited
Regent's Wharf
All Saints Street
London N1 9PA

Phaidon Press Inc.
65 Bleecker Street
New York, NY 10012

phaidon.com

First published 2016
© 2016 Phaidon Press Limited

ISBN 978 0 7148 7119 6

A CIP catalogue record for this book
is available from the British Library.

Designed by Julia Hasting
Printed in Italy

With thanks to Deb Aaronson,
Dave Bell, Christian Bunyan,
Victoria Clarke, Tim Cooke, Sanne
van Ettinger, Kara Fraser, João Mota,
Michael Moynihan, Alenka Oblak,
Rosie Pickles, Laurie Robins and
Anthony Sarchiapone for bringing
this book to fruition.

Picture Credits
Unless otherwise stated all images
are courtesy Erik Kessels. Any
inadvertent omissions can be
rectified in future editions. Courtesy
Lucas Blalock: 135–7; © Heike
Bollig, (Jar, 2008; Book, 2004; Dice,
2006; 3 pink balloons, 2005; Marble,
2009; Screw, 2004; Pretzel stick,
2006; Teabag, 2005), c/o Pictoright
Amsterdam, 2015: 37–41; Courtesy
Kurt Caviezel: 93–7; Courtesy
Daniel Eatock: 26–7; Courtesy Hans
Eijkelboom: 138–142; Courtesy
Joan Fontcuberta: 145–9; Erik
Kessels, In almost every picture #9,
KesselsKramer Publishing, 2010:
78–82, 84; Erik Kessels, In almost
every picture #13, KesselsKramer
Publishing, 2014: 52–4, 56; Erik
Kessels, Sabine Verschueren, Hans
Wolf and André Thijssen, Wonder,
2006: 7, 42–6, 166; Courtesy Daniel
Pario Perra: 102–3; Peter Piller: 160;
PUTPUT: 106–7; Kent Rogowski:
111–12; Joachim Schmid: 153–5;
Helmut Smits: 105; Photograph ©
Matt Stuart: 66–8; Photograph ©
André Thijssen: 2, 71–4; Courtesy
Ruth van Beek: 121–3.

D0051188